WAY

YOUNG PROFILES

Will Smith

Paul Joseph
ABDO Publishing Company

visit us at
www.abdopub.com

Published by ABDO Publishing Company 4940 Viking Drive, Edina, Minnesota 55435.
Copyright © 1999 by Abdo Consulting Group, Inc. International copyrights reserved in
all countries. No part of this book may be reproduced in any form without written
permission from the publisher.

Printed in the United States.
Photo credits: AP/Wide World; Shooting Star
Edited by Tamara L. Britton
Contributing editor A.T. McKenna

To my nephew John (Will Smith's #1 fan)

Library of Congress Cataloging-in-Publication Data

Joseph, Paul, 1970-
    Will Smith / Paul Joseph.
    p. cm. -- (Young profiles)
    Includes index.
    Summary: Highlights the personal life and successful musical and acting career
    of the Grammy-winning rap singer and star of his own television series and such
    hit movies as "Independence Day" and "Men in Black."
    ISBN 1-57765-320-3 (hardcover)
    ISBN 1-57765-332-7 (paperback)
    1. Smith, Will, 1968- --Juvenile literature. 2. Motion Picture actors and
    actresses-- United States--Biography--Juvenile literature. [1. Smith, Will, 1968-
    2. Actors and actresses. 3. Rap musicians. 4. Afro-Americans--Biography.] I.
    Title. II. Series.
    PN2287.S612J67   1999
    791.43'028'092--dc21
    [B]   98-39495
                                                               CIP
                                                               AC

Contents

Big Willie Style

Will Smith has gone by many different names. From the Fresh Prince to Mr. Smith to Big Will to his newest nickname Big Willie. None of these snazzy names can begin to fully describe one of the most talented entertainers in the world.

Will Smith is one of the most popular actors in Hollywood. But this mega-talent isn't just an actor. He is also a great musician. Will is the only person in history to have blockbuster films, a top-rated television show, and three **Grammy awards**—all by the age of 28!

Will's bright eyes, winning smile, and wonderful sense of humor appeal to people of all ages and backgrounds. He first dazzled people with his talent in 1988 with his partner "DJ Jazzy" Jeff Townes. At that time, Will was known as the Fresh Prince. The two made history by winning the first Grammy ever presented for **rap music**.

Will's appeal in rap led to NBC giving him his own sitcom. *The Fresh Prince of Bel Air* was a popular hit for six seasons. After making it big in both music and television, it was on to the movies where he became one of Hollywood's leading men.

Whether it is music, television, or the movies, Will Smith is the best in the business. And he does it with his own distinctive style—Big Willie style!

Will Smith, right, holds the Grammy for Best Rap Solo for the song "Men In Black" as DJ Jazzy Jeff looks on at the 40th Annual Grammy Awards.

Profile of Big Willie

Name: Willard C. Smith II

Birth Date: September 25, 1968

Place of Birth: Philadelphia, Pennsylvania

Height: 6 feet, 2 inches

Weight: 206 pounds

Parents: Carolyn and Willard Smith, Sr.

Siblings: Pam, Ellen, and Harry

Job: **Rapper**, actor

Marital Status: Divorced from Sheree Zampino; married to actress Jada Pinkett

Children: Son, Willard C. Smith III, nicknamed Trey, born in December 1992; son, Jaden, born July 1998

Pets: Four rottweiler dogs

Hobbies: Golfing, shooting pool, playing basketball and chess

Favorite Athlete: Julius "Dr. J" Erving (basketball legend who played for the Philadelphia 76ers)

Favorite Actors: Eddie Murphy, Bill Cosby

Favorite Musicians: The Fugees, Biggie Smalls, LL Cool J, and Run DMC

Quote From Will: "There are individual personality traits of celebrities and sports stars and people whom I admire. But the only people I idolize are my parents."

The Man in Black—Big Willie!

Willie From Philly

Willard C. Smith II was born September 25, 1968, in West Philadelphia, Pennsylvania. Will, or Willie as he was known, was born to a working-class household. His father, Willard Sr., was a refrigeration engineer and his mother, Carolyn, was a school administrator.

Will is the second of four children. He has an older sister, Pam, and two younger siblings, twins Ellen and Harry. His parents were very strict and believed in teaching good values to their children. They also believed that children should have a lot of fun.

Even as a young boy, Will loved to laugh and entertain people. He was a friendly, likable, and smart child who had a lot of friends. Will loved to perform for his siblings and friends by making faces and getting them into all kinds of trouble for laughing at him at places like school and church!

As a child, Will appeared in several church and school plays and pageants. Even at a young age people could sense a talented young actor. Will could easily memorize his lines and he wasn't afraid to perform in front of a large group.

Besides acting, Will's interests included dinosaurs, sports, science, math, and especially music. Will took piano lessons and was very good. Will's parents also stressed the importance of studying hard and getting a good education.

Will is from West Philadelphia.

DJ Jazzy Jeff and The Fresh Prince

Will attended Our Lady of Lourdes, a Catholic junior high school. For high school, Will attended Overbrook High, a public school. There, Will was best known for his charm and fun personality.

Since Will was so nice and could talk his way out of any situation, his teachers nicknamed him Prince Charming. The name caught on and soon everyone referred to Will by the shorter version of Prince. Will liked the nickname, but added "Fresh" before the Prince to give it a little more spice.

Although Will was known as the class clown and could make anyone laugh, including his teachers, he still got excellent grades. Will was especially good in science and math. After high school Will was offered a scholarship to attend MIT (Massachusetts Institute of Technology), one of the finest **colleges** in the country.

Fate, however, would lead him down a different path. When Will was 12 years old he was at a birthday party. He was the center of attention by clowning around and making people laugh. Jeff Townes was watching Will and thought Will was the funniest guy he had ever seen. He immediately went over to see Will and the two hit it off.

DJ Jazzy Jeff and the Fresh Prince.

Jeff was a **DJ** and Will was a **rapper**. Both boys were very talented. Throughout high school they played at parties and clubs and had a large following. DJ Jazzy Jeff and the Fresh Prince were born and the two would go on to make history.

Parents Just Don't Understand

What started as fun for Will and Jeff turned into a very **profitable** business. In 1985, when Will was just 16, a small-time **record producer** heard the duo at a club and asked them if they would like to make a record. Soon their single "Girls Ain't Nothing But Trouble" was being played throughout Philadelphia.

A representative from Jive Records heard the single, and offered to release it nationwide. Will was very excited. He thought he would just enjoy it for awhile and then go off to **college**. The song was being played everywhere and became a hit. Although Will's parents were upset, he decided not to go to MIT and instead concentrate on music.

Shortly after graduating from high school in 1986, DJ Jazzy Jeff and the Fresh Prince began touring the country and playing their music. In 1987, the duo's first album, *Rock the House*, hit the charts and instantly went gold.

The following year, their second album, *He's the DJ, I'm the Rapper* had the hit single "Parents Just Don't Understand." It sold three million copies. The song made the duo the most popular entertainers of the year.

Will and Jeff had earned a place in music history. Due to the success of DJ Jazzy Jeff and the Fresh Prince, the **Grammy** committee created a new category: Best Rap Performance. Will and Jeff received the first rap Grammy ever! By now, Will's parents just had to understand why he chose a music career.

Will Smith winning another Grammy Award.

From Riches to Rags

Will and Jeff were two of the hottest entertainers in the world and they were only teenagers! When they came back to Philadelphia, fans, family, and even the mayor greeted them at the airport. The duo was on top of the world.

All of the money, awards, and fame soon went to Will's head and he began to make many foolish mistakes. He had made millions of dollars, but had spent it quickly. Will bought a mansion in Philadelphia, two motorcycles, and six new cars. He went on shopping sprees and took trips with friends all over the world, and he always paid.

By 1989, Will was flat broke. Will's father was very upset with his son and let him know. When Will once bragged to his dad about his many cars and motorcycles, his father replied, "What do you need six cars and two motorcycles for when you only have one butt!?"

Will learned his lesson and quickly grew up. It took him over three years to pay off all of his debt and his back taxes. "In life there are two types of people: those who make mistakes, and keep making the same mistakes over and over again, and those who learn from their mistakes. I like to think I'm the latter," Will said.

Jazzy Jeff (L) and Will Smith were the hottest entertainers in the world at one time.

The Fresh Prince of Bel Air

Will got focused and decided that he would concentrate on music. He learned his lesson about money and foolish spending. In 1991, he and Jeff recorded the album, *Homebase*, which featured the hit song "Summertime."

The album sold over two million copies and earned them another **Grammy** for Best Rap Performance by a Duo or Group. By now though, Will was interested in acting. Will loved his life as a **rapper**, but also wanted to become an actor.

It was apparent in his videos that Will was a natural actor. He decided to move from Philadelphia to Hollywood to give acting a chance. Benny Medina and Quincy Jones came up with the concept for a show about a young, poor African American who would move in with his rich relatives and go to an exclusive private school.

Medina and Jones both thought Will would be perfect as the lead character. First though, Will had to audition in front of the **executives** at NBC. Will picked up the script and read life into lines that he had never seen before. The executives were very impressed.

NBC executives had found a natural actor and their next prime-time star. Will Smith became the lead in *The Fresh Prince of Bel Air*. Soon every magazine and newspaper in the country was talking about this new show and this great, new, young actor. The show became an instant hit.

Will as the Fresh Prince of Bel Air.

From Prime-Time to Big Screen

The *Fresh Prince of Bel Air* premiered in the fall of 1990. It quickly became the number one show in its time slot. Year after year it maintained its high ratings.

Will didn't forget about his music or his best friend Jeff. For most of the six-year run of the show, Jeff would often appear as Will's buddy Jazz. In the summer, the duo worked on new music.

In 1991, just one year after the show first aired, Will was offered the lead in the movie *House Party*. Will turned down the offer because he felt he wasn't ready for the big screen.

Will knew that he wanted to be in movies, but he wanted to take it slow. In 1992, Will was in his first movie, *Where the Day Takes You*. It was a small role in a low-budget film. Will learned a lot about the movie business and loved it.

In 1993, he got a small part in a big film called *Made in America*. It starred Ted Danson and Whoopi Goldberg.

Although Will did a good job in the movie, people still wondered why he kept taking such small parts. Will didn't give in to the pressure to take larger roles. He wanted to make sure that he was ready. After his next movie, everyone knew that he could be a leading man.

A scene from Fresh Prince of Bel Air.

Movie Star

In 1993, Will was cast in the movie *Six Degrees of Separation*. He played a con-man who talked his way into the homes of rich people. It was a serious role for Will and most people didn't think he could handle it. But once again, Will proved his **critics** wrong. People now knew that Will was a true movie star.

During this time, Will got married and became a father. After dating for a year, Will and his girlfriend Sheree Zampino were married in May of 1992. In December of 1992, the couple became the proud parents of Willard C. Smith III, whom they nicknamed Trey.

Will continued to work on the show, his movies, and his music. But all of the time away from his family was starting to take its toll. It was hard on Sheree not seeing her husband for weeks at time.

In 1995, Sheree filed for divorce. The divorce shattered Will. For the first time, he felt he had failed at something. "I really believe that a man and woman together, raising a family, is the purest form of happiness we can experience, and I messed that up," said Will.

Will never blamed Sheree for leaving. He knew that he didn't pay enough attention to his family. "The breakup wasn't the perfect situation and it isn't what I wanted but I still have the most beautiful thing I have ever seen in my life and that is my son."

A scene from Six Degrees of Separation.

Blockbuster Mega-Star

After his success in *Six Degrees of Separation*, Will wanted to concentrate more on movies. He decided it was time to end the hit show *The Fresh Prince of Bel Air*. Although he wanted to work on movies, he also wanted to end his show on top. *The Fresh Prince of Bel Air* was in the top ten most of its six seasons.

Soon came his first leading role in a movie. Will and Martin Lawrence starred in the movie *Bad Boys*. The two actors were great together. The action-buddy cop movie earned a whopping $140 million. It turned out to be one of the biggest box-office hits of 1995.

Bad Boys was only the beginning for Will. By 1995, Will had everything. He had **Grammy awards** and the lead in a hit television show. He had proved he was a great actor in *Six Degrees of Separation,* and *Bad Boys* showed that he could draw big crowds. But what happened next no one would have dreamed—not even the confident Will.

Will Smith playing the lead role in the movie Bad Boys.

ID4 and MIB

Right after *Bad Boys*, Will was cast in the movie *Independence Day (ID4)*. In this movie, Will played Captain Steven Hill, a fighter pilot who saves the world from an alien attack. *ID4* was a hit all around the world with its scary premise, amazing special effects, and great cast. It was 1996's biggest movie, raking in over $800 million worldwide!

After *ID4* everyone wanted Will Smith in their movies, including one of the greatest **directors** in the world—Steven Spielberg. Spielberg has created some of the biggest movies of all time including *E.T.* and *Jurassic Park*. Spielberg wanted Will for the lead in *Men in Black (MIB)*. Will jumped at the chance.

Will Smith, wearing military fatigues, at the premiere of Independence Day, *with fellow cast members.*

Opposite page: Will (L) and Tommy Lee Jones, getting slimed in the movie Men in Black.

24

Will played Agent J and Tommy Lee Jones played Agent K. The two were special agents who were cracking down on illegal aliens—from outer space! *MIB* also included some amazing special effects.

Exactly one year after *Independence Day* opened, *Men in Black* premiered. It was the biggest hit of the year, earning over $300 million! The movie also brought Will back to the recording studio to record a couple of songs for the movie soundtrack. The songs "Men in Black" and "Just Cruisin' " became major hits. It also earned Will another **Grammy** for Best Rap Solo performance.

Big Willie's Gettin' Jiggy

Will was now one of the biggest entertainers in the world. But it was his music that gave him his start and he was ready to go back. In 1997, Will put out his first solo album, *Big Willie Style*. The album included the hit song, "Gettin' Jiggy Wit' It."

Will was excited to be rapping again. After four years of being away from the music world, many thought he would be rusty. But not Will Smith. Rhymes still rolled off his tongue and he was better than ever.

On December 31, 1997, Will married his girlfriend Jada Pinkett. In July 1998, the couple had a baby boy named Jaden. Will is happier than ever. He has a wonderful wife, two beautiful children, and is one of the hottest entertainers in the world.

Will Smith soared onto the music charts just 10 years ago. He jumped over to television in the blink of an eye. After having a hit show, Will slowly became a blockbuster mega-star. And now he has done a full circle and made another hit album.

What more can Will possibly do? According to Will, a lot. After another hit movie, *Enemy of the State*, Will signed on to do *Bad Boys 2*, and *Wild Wild West*. Will also wants to keep rapping and making music, and perhaps someday direct and produce movies. Most of all Will wants to be a good father and husband. His goal is to be as good at it as his own parents were.

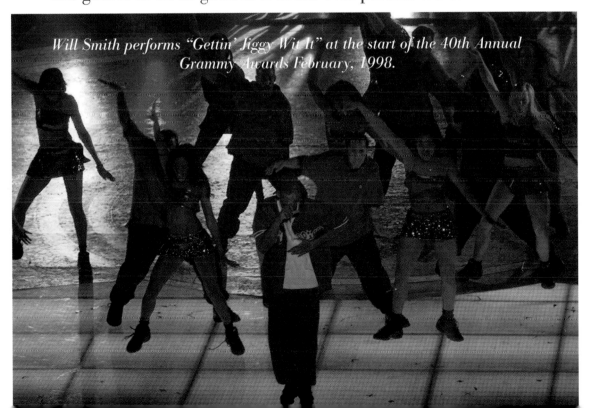

Will Smith performs "Gettin' Jiggy Wit It" at the start of the 40th Annual Grammy Awards February, 1998.

Fun Facts on Big Willie

Awards and Honors

Grammy Award: 1988, 1991, 1998

MTV Music Video Award: 1989

American Music Award: 1988, 1991

NAACP Image Award for Television: 1992

NAACP Image Award for Music: 1992

Blockbuster Entertainment Award: 1997

Nickelodeon Kids' Choice Award: 1997

MTV Movie Award: 1997

MTV Music Award: 1997, 1998

People's Choice Award: 1997

VH1 Fashion Award: 1997

Will Smith mocks tears as he accepts his award for Best Fight in a movie for his bout with a giant cockroach in Men in Black.

Albums

Rock the House (1987)

He's the DJ, I'm the Rapper (1988)

And In This Corner (1989)

Homebase (1991)

Code Red (1993)

Men in Black (1997)

Big Willie Style (1997)

Television

The Fresh Prince of Bel Air (1990 -96)

Movies

Where the Day Takes You (1992)

Made in America (1993)

Six Degrees of Separation (1993)

Bad Boys (1995)

Independence Day (1996)

Men In Black (1997)

Enemy of the State (1998)

Glossary

College: a school that a person goes to after graduating from high school to receive a degree in a specialized field.

Critic: a person who judges different artistic works such as music, movies, television, etc.

Director: a person who is in charge of making a performance such as a television show or movie by organizing, supervising, and making most of the decisions about the performance.

DJ: the person in rap music who is in charge of making the music by "scratching" records on a turntable.

Executives: people who are in charge of making the decisions in different businesses.

Grammy Award: the highest award that can be given to musicians.

Profitable: something that makes a lot of money.

Rap Music: a type of music that is accompanied by background music and lyrics that usually rhyme.

Rapper: a person in rap music who writes and sings the lyrics.

Record Producer: a person who is in charge of putting an album or a single together.

Will on the Web

Will's Official Webpage:

www.willsmith.net

The Last Word From Will

On Why Americans Love Him So Much: "It's the ears! Americans have an ear fetish. Absolutely. Americans love people with big ears—Mickey Mouse, Goofy, Dumbo. Americans love ears."

Pass It On

Tell readers around the country information you've learned about your favorite superstars. Share your little-known facts and interesting stories.
We want to hear from you!
To get posted on the ABDO Publishing Company Web site, E-mail us at "Adventure@abdopub.com"
Download a free screen saver at www.abdopub.com

Index